SUCCESS IS NEVER PAVED!

Dr. Kevin C. Snyder

Thank you,

Kevin

Copyright 2012 © by Inspir-Active Solutions

ISBN-13: 978-1479254149
ISBN-10: 1479254142

Library of Congress Cataloging-in-Publication Data:
Snyder, Kevin Charles.
   Success is Never Paved!

   1)   Motivational and Inspirational
            SEL021000
   2)   Personal Growth
            SEL031000
   3)   Leadership
            EDU032000

Editing, Layout and Design by Inspir-Active Solutions and its associates.

For additional information, contact:
Email: Kevin@KevinCSnyder.com
Web: www.KevinCSnyder.com

To become a published author by contributing a chapter in the 'Leading the Way' book series, please contact: Kevin@InspirActiveSolutions.com

Contents

SUCCESS IS NEVER PAVED!

Dr. Kevin C. Snyder

Introduction

Success is Never Paved! is a collection of leadership lessons and inspirational true stories that address a variety of dynamic topics for impacting positive change and growth in any arena of life. There is not just one way to achieve success and we all define success differently and in our own unique way. Success is never achieved in the same manner; hence – it's never, ever paved! By taking a few moments to read this content, the lens at which you look at life and your attitude toward obstacles will forever be changed. As you read this book, open your mind to absorb and understand the true meaning of these experiences, successes, failures, and hardships.

Success does leave clues and mistakes should be considered lessons of wisdom. Nothing has meaning except the meaning we give it. Each chapter captures an authentic essence and philosophy of leadership that has the potential to catapult your success. However, for these accomplishments to manifest, you have to be intentional about having high expectations from this book and be willing to work diligently. As I say when I begin every keynote speech, "Life has a tendency to live up to the expectations we have for it." So 'expect' to be empowered, transformed, and enlightened about various leadership topics that will change your life in every way.

Thank you for investing time to read

Success is Never Paved!

To Your Continued Success,

Dr. Kevin C. Snyder

Motivational Speaker, Author and Entrepreneur

Kevin@InspirActiveSolutions.com

"Life has a tendency to live up
to the expectations we have for it."

THE COMMON DENOMINATOR OF SUCCESS

My goal for you is that after reading this chapter, you will become amazingly aware of just how close you already are to extraordinary success. Your breakthrough moment is just about to happen and this content will help you ignite that extra energy to manifest your desired goals.

I have always been fascinated by *how* and *why* some people achieve so much success. I have read hundreds of leadership books, interviewed dozens of incredibly successful people, and learned from many extraordinary mentors. My own doctoral research was focused on positive psychology and how one's personal belief system impacted their ability to succeed and achieve goals. From what I have experienced and studied, I am convinced about one common element in the success equation for attaining amazing results and fulfillment in life.

There is a common denominator amongst all successful people who have achieved greatness.

The greatest achievers of all time demonstrate many unique and diverse talents, characteristics, and pathways. Yet one specific quality stands as a proven commonality amongst each of them. But before sharing this principle, let me provide a few examples:

- Thomas Edison envisioned and created many inventions, one of them being the light bulb operated by electricity. Despite nearly 10,000 failures and mistakes in which it would not work, he persisted until he found a way to make the light bulb a physical success.

- The Wright brothers, dreaming of flight, repeatedly altered their 'flying machine' and experienced hundreds of unsuccessful attempts before finally flying through the air and changing history.

- Jack Canfield and Mark Victor Hansen, co-founders and authors of *Chicken Soup for the Soul*, were turned down by 132 publishers before the next publisher finally 'gave them a break.' Now, over 120 million *Chicken Soup* books have been sold across the world in 40 languages.

- Basketball legend, Michael Jordan, was cut from his junior high school basketball team because 'he wasn't good enough yet.' Afterwards, he practiced every day for a year at home and successfully tried out again one year later. The rest of his story is beyond amazing.

So what do these great achievers above have in common? What is their common denominator for extraordinary success?

The commonality that these individuals possess, as well as other successful leaders, is that they simply persisted. They did not quit when faced with an obstacle or set back. Rather, they kept trying until they finally found a way to make their dream come true.

These individuals did not hear 'No' for an answer. Instead, they only heard "Not yet' or 'Not this way.' They learned from each mistake and obstacle instead of giving up or believing that someone else was in charge of their destiny. They had passion and they persisted until circumstances became favorable.

> *Great achievers don't hear 'No.'*
> *They only hear 'Not yet' or 'Not this way.'*
> *Successful people view setbacks as set-ups!*

What is remarkable about this common denominator theme of persistence is that it is no secret. Anyone can achieve greatness if they believe strongly enough in their dream and take action repeatedly until it finally manifests in their life. Success truly occurs when preparation meets opportunity. However, sometimes that opportunity or ideal circumstance is days, months, or even years away. Yet if we truly have a healthy, authentic passion towards a goal or idea, then we WANT to persist and we WANT to break through barriers. Pursuing a passionate goal isn't a chore. And that my friends, is the secret to success and the key to true serenity in life. Achieving goals is one thing – overcoming obstacles is fulfillment and life satisfaction.

For no other reason, YOU will be successful because when others quit, YOU don't. Your persistence alone will dictate your success. Think about the examples I have provided above. If Jack Canfield and Mar Victor Hansen had stopped at the 10th or 130th publisher, then we would not have *Chicken Soup for the Soul*. If the Wright Brothers or Thomas Edison had not continued adapting their inventions, then we might not have electric light or flight in the way we know it today.

Passion is essential but persistence is key. Continued action despite setbacks and obstacles will determine your achievement and success. An invincible determination can accomplish anything.

> *For no other reason, you'll be successful because when other people quit, YOU don't.*

You never lose unless you give up. And you don't measure success by how many times you get knocked down; rather, you measure success by how many times you get up. Everyone gets knocked down at some point.

As I work with clients to present keynote and leadership workshops across the country, I have fallen in love with one particular 'power question' which changes people's lives. It is an introspective question and requires that you truly focus on your life and experiences. That question is:

What are you most proud about?

Take a moment to reflect on your most proud accomplishment in your life. You might have several, which is wonderful, but at least identify one. Recall what that proudest experience was. Vision it and feel the emotions that it brings to you.

Again, what are you most proud about in your life?

Do not continue reading until you have identified at least one accomplishment ...

I always hear fascinating responses to this question, whether they are one-on-one coaching sessions or responses in large group presentations. I absolutely love hearing what others are most proud about.

Here's the catch – without even knowing you, I am 110% confident that the accomplishment you identified involved sacrifice, hard work and dedication. I also believe your achievement was a direct result of significant effort over a long period of time and was not a result of something that simply resulted overnight.

Together, you and I have just realized the common denominator success secret for living a fulfilled life. Our greatest accomplishments do not result from luck, being in the right place at the right time, or who we know. Rather, our most proud experiences result from us sacrificing for what we desire most and by taking persistent action over and over again.

> *The things most important to us are also the things we have to work the hardest for.*

Of course we want things to be easy rather than difficult. Even for myself, I don't necessarily want my goals to be frustrating and full of obstacles. However, if it was easy, then everyone would be doing it. I know that in order for me to be successful, persistence is a part of the success equation. I'll be successful because when other people quit, I don't.

When we do encounter obstacles or frustrations, how do we respond? Do we give up or press onward? Our society has become too entitled with expecting instant success and gratification. We feel that if we don't get what we want on the first attempt, then it is not meant to be. That mentality is not the inner voice of winner – that is the voice of a whiner. Know what you want and go get it.

Let's continue with more personal examples …

- How did you learn to swim or ride a bicycle?
- How did you learn to walk as a child?
- If you wanted to lose weight right now, become more fit or build muscle, how would you do that?

In the themed spirit of persistence, clearly the answer is that you achieved these things, or would achieve these things, by continued effort over a period of time. And many times, you were helped, or would be helped, and encouraged along the way. By not giving up, success occurs. Anything of true, genuine importance in life comes from a passionate desire and persistence.

How many attempts will you take towards your dream, towards an idea that others may or may not believe in? Will you be like Jack Canfield and Mark Victor Hansen, Thomas Edison, and Michael Jordan, or will you expect the easy route in life and stop when things get tough? These examples I have shared, and there are thousands more, are individuals no better than you or I. Rather, these individuals just kept persisting beyond ordinary and believed in themselves and their dream.

Again, the reason you'll be successful, for no other reason, is that when others quit, you don't. Persistence is the common denominator secret of success.

CREATE THE CIRCUMSTANCES YOU WANT!

I recently received a call from a friend, Sarah, whom I had unfortunately lost touch with since my move to North Carolina from Florida. She called to thank me for helping her vision a goal that had just manifested in her life.

Last year, Sarah's company hosted a competition where they were awarding an all-expenses-paid trip to Paris for the top earning account executive and their guest. Sarah, being one of the youngest and newest members of the team, also had an incredibly diligent work ethic and passionate drive for her work. And most importantly, she believed and had faith she could win that trip to Paris if she worked hard enough.

When Sarah told me about the competition, I remember observing the conviction in her eyes and the hunger to win that award. She truly did envision going to Paris on the company's dime rather than just 'hope' to win and travel there. Sarah understood the difference between hoping something would happen and creating the circumstances in life to make it happen.

> *Some people in life make things happen, others watch things happen, and some unfortunately wonder, 'What just happened?'*

So when Sarah told me about this exciting opportunity and asked for suggestions, I recommended to her that she think of a creative way to be reminded of and visualize winning that trip to Paris. Meaning, I wanted her to find a symbolic way to envision Paris each and every day until it manifested for her.

Sarah and I lost touch after that conversation due to the fact that I moved several states away. To be honest, I completely forgot about our Paris conversation and never followed up with her to hear the outcome.

When Sarah recently called me though, here's how the conversation about Paris transpired:

"Kevin," she said. "Do you remember that conversation we had about Paris last year and how badly I wanted to win that trip from my company?"

"Oh yeah, I sure do," I replied. "What ever happened?"

"Well," she said. "I just got back from Paris! I took my brother on the trip and it was phenomenal!"

"That is fantastic! Congratulations! I'm so proud of you." I said.

She continued, "I'm calling to thank you for helping me win that award. You made it possible and helped me believe in that dream coming to reality. Thank you."

"What are you talking about Sarah? You did all the work. I just had a conversation with you about it over a year ago."

"But you helped me vision it and that's why I won," she said. "If it were not for your idea to find that daily reminder of winning, I don't think I would have been as motivated. It was on my mind every day and helped me believe I deserved to win. So thank you!'

"Well," I replied. "I defer all credit back to you, but thank you for believing in the visualization process. It's powerful isn't it? I'm so happy for you Sarah."

Sarah and I continued our conversation for several more minutes and she shared details about what specifically she did to remind her of Paris on a daily basis. Unbeknownst to me until that conversation, Sarah took two significant actions which led to her ultimate success. The first being that she created a goal board, commonly known as a vision board, with a list of all her goals and expectations she desired to come to fruition that year. She took clippings and pictures from magazines, typed and printed off her own phrases, and even put tangible symbols of items and pinned them to a piece of cork board. One of those items on her board was a picture of the Eiffel Tower with a typed phrase underneath reading, 'Congratulations, You Won the Trip To Paris!' Her vision board was that simple and took her only two hours to create.

The second vital action she took was buying a mini, one-inch Eiffel Tower key chain. Like her vision board, this figurative key chain was a symbolic, hourly reminder of not just Paris but more importantly winning her company's award. She knew she could travel to Paris at any time, but she wanted the satisfaction and fulfillment knowing it was an award from her company. Therefore, each time she grasped her keys to travel from appointment to appointment she would see that Eiffel Tower and be reminded about working even harder to win Paris.

> *"You must see your goals clearly and specifically before you can set out for them. Hold them in your mind until they become second nature."*
> *- Les Brown*

It is critically important to acknowledge that Sarah also worked diligently hard and was extremely persistent to win that Paris award. She also possessed an internal belief system which allowed her to believe she could beat the more experienced competition. But according to Sarah, what helped her the most was visualizing Paris as a goal already achieved through her vision board and key chain. Those two symbols of achievement helped her to daydream with a purpose and activate her creative power of what I call 'intentional realization'. Quite simply, Sarah saw Paris not as what it could be, but as what it would be. She created and visualized the circumstances she wanted.

How often do you visualize goals like Sarah? When is the last time you allowed yourself to confidently daydream about a desire manifesting in your life? What is an exciting achievement you hope might someday happen but you never have done anything about it yet? If you are waiting for the ideal circumstance, how's that working for you?

Unfortunately for most of us, it has been a long time since we have allowed ourselves the creative freedom to listen to our hearts desires. We aspire for and envy significant accomplishments but we do not feel deserving of having such wonderful achievement. And with a seemingly lofty goal where we honestly have no clue where to start, we settle for never taking any action. Furthermore, we convince ourselves that circumstances need to be more ideal before we make any important decisions. As a result, we never fully experience the magnitude of greatness that exists in our lives and in the lives of others.

Leaders take action. Extraordinary leaders feel the fear and do it anyway. They create the circumstances they want!

So stop being destructive to yourself. I give you permission right now to only be creatively constructive. Identify a goal that has always been a 'What If?' in your life and start visualizing it in your life. You deserve it. Do what Sarah did and take time to create a vision board and find a symbol that can serve as a daily reminder for what will come, not what might come. If you don't do it, who will? As I have shared in previous column issues, the best way to do something is to start doing it. Achievement and greatness like never before are waiting for you to believe and act.

Imagination is the preview to life's coming attractions.
~ Einstein

EVERY SETBACK IS A SET-UP

A fascinating concept is that our lives have a tendency to live up to the expectations we have for it. Our dominant thoughts perpetuate our reality. Therefore, this year could still be the best year of your life simply because you choose for it to be from this moment forward. The formula is quite simple -- choose your thoughts to change your life!

The truth is that most people get temporarily motivated and set some sort of resolution or goal only at the new year. Interestingly though, research has shown that within 30 days, by February, 85% of those who have set a resolution are already NOT continuing it.

Here is a simple, easy-to-remember success formula about life: *To make a life change, you must choose to make a 'life-style' change.* And it is imperative that you truly desire and believe in a 'life-style' change so much it compels you to take intentional action. The unfortunate challenge is that many of us have ignored, or are not aware, of what these desires in our heart and mind actually are. We have become so fast-paced and routine that we robotically go through each day focused on our responsibilities and possibly a paycheck.

But today is a new day and an opportunity to live abundantly without limits. You can achieve this by doing one thing – *By Following Your PASSION!*

Pursuing your passion is the essential *sine qua non* secret to success and living without limits. Decide now to make this the best year of your life by finally following your authentic passion. Passion is what fuels your soul and mind with boundless energy to impact positive change. Motivation is only temporary -- passion is limitless!

Most people do not set a goal or resolution they are passion about. Rather, they pick a goal that sounds positive or perhaps something they think they want or that is good for them. A successful 'life-style' change requires passion, commitment, and many times sacrifice. Therefore, it is essential that you only set goals you are passionate about because that passion will fuel your persistence through obstacles and setbacks. "When you have passion for something, you find a way to make it happen." – Zig Ziglar

Think of someone in your life whom you feel is extremely successful? Vision that person in your mind right now and mentally identify the top reasons why you believe they are so accomplished. I am confident that a common denominator for all your reasoning is that the person you identified as successful is PASSIONATE about many things – their family, their work, and life overall. And through this passion, they are magnetic to be around and have also overcome tremendous adversity in their lives. *Am I correct?*

So how do you just follow your passion? How do you know what your true passion might be?

Success strategy one: Ask yourself, what desire captures your interest and makes your heart smile? What makes time stop when you even think about doing it?

<u>Success strategy two</u>: Ask yourself, what are you good at? What do you enjoy doing?

By reflecting on the answers for these two success strategies above, you will come to identify your true passions. When you envision following them, you will begin to feel a desire so powerful in your mind that your body swells with energy and you mentally picture these goals and dreams already manifesting in your life. The next step is to allow yourself to savor the anticipation of these passions becoming exciting realities. Enjoy the beginning journey of making 2012 the best year of your life!

> *"All achievement first begins with an intense, burning desire for something definite."*
> *– Napolean Hill*

Some of you might be wondering 'how do I do this when I have so much responsibility and so little time?'

Do not yet focus on 'how' you will accomplish these passions and goals yet. In fact, do not even question whether they are truly attainable. For now, just focus on the feeling and belief that the 'how' will show up. Begin spending 15-30 minutes each day on these newly revealed passions and goals. I have an entire chapter of my book 'Think Differently', which outlines this strategy - and it works.

I acknowledge that we all have different circumstances, and some of us have more 'responsibility' than others which might limit how much risk we can take to follow our passions and make a personal, life change. But that does not mean we cannot make a change; rather, it just means that we must consider these 'responsibilities' as we move forward toward manifesting those things we are passionate about in our lives. Where some can make a 10 degree change, others can only make a 1-2 degree change. The amount of degree is irrelevant; what matters is the effort and action of simply beginning.

> *Each day, you should spend 15-30 minutes on something you are interested in and passionate about.*

So instead of saying 'No, I have too much responsibility,' ask yourself 'How can I manage my responsibilities and still achieve my desires?' When you ask yourself 'how,' it eliminates the excuses and opens our mind to creatively find the answers.

I believe the secret key to living without limits and unlocking all life has to offer is understanding PASSION and how it relates to our lives. Everyone has access to this key; in fact, they hold it in their hands each day. Unfortunately, most do not know they hold it so closely, if at all. The *secret* is that it's *not a secret*.

When you have passion for something, you find a way to make it happen. If you're not passionate about your goal, then don't waste your time! What you think about you bring about. Your life perpetuates what your mind focuses on most. So think positive and THINK abundance. VISION abundance. EXPECT and SAVOR the anticipation for receiving abundance! NOW is your time. This is your year.

The greatest legacy is not what we leave FOR people, but what we leave IN people. Identify and follow your passions and inspire those around you to do the same. Passion is the key to fulfillment. This will be the best year of your life because you choose for it to be.

It's Not What We Need to **LEARN**, It's What We Need to **UNLEARN**!

As often as possible, I enjoy asking the following question both during my leadership seminars and individually with my coaching clients. I simply ask, 'By show of hands (or individually), who here has ever had a thought?'

People typically then smile, chuckle in response, and then look at me as if I just landed from Planet Zorkon. Sometimes, I even see a few eyes roll or heads inquisitively scan the room in quest to observe responses from others. Interestingly, people seem to be uncomfortable answering that simple question! I will acknowledge though, that asking 'Who here has ever had a thought?' might seem like a silly or meaningless question to pose. However, think about *why* I would ask that question for a moment. That's right - think about why you would think about a thought.

Here is the point: It is impossible to not have thoughts. In fact, we have hundreds, if not thousands of thoughts every single day. And each thought is a powerful inner voice that guides and shapes our feelings which resultantly leads to our choices, behaviors, and outcomes. That inner voice chatter is sometimes positive and sometimes negative; sometimes constructive and sometimes destructive. Our self-talk is potently commanding and it is the core source of energy that services the operating system for the most powerful computer in the world – our brain!

But more importantly, here is the meaning: We have spent out entire lives conditioning our minds to think a certain way. We have literally programmed our brains, again the most powerful information processors in the world, to believe certain things as well as to *not* believe certain things; on how to communicate; on how to react, etc. Without being employed by any Geek Squad, we have built a computer operating system that has conditioned our lives for both success and failure in life.

When we accomplish a goal, our behaviors and beliefs that led to achieving that success are affirmed, whether we acknowledge that cognitive realization or not. And when we are empowered by someone who encourages us, that positive discourse is also engrained in our belief system that we can achieve whatever that goal is we set. Verbal persuasion, social reinforcement, and performance accomplishments are all foundational elements that build self-efficacy which is the genesis formulating our belief system. A strong level of self-efficacy suggests that we believe we can accomplish the goals we set for ourselves whereas a negative sense of efficacy suggests the opposite.

> *It's not what we need to learn, it's what we need to unlearn to unleash our true potential!*

So many times in life, most specifically in relationships and in organizational leadership, it is not what we need to learn, it is what we need to unlearn to achieve the results we want. We must continually keep programming our minds on what is possible rather than what is not, on reasons why we should work toward a goal rather than on excuses why we should not. Successful people share many common characteristics and one signature quality is that they see opportunities and possibilities not through sight, but rather through the power of their mind.

Leaders envision a goal manifesting in their life before it actually does. They do not wait for every condition to be exactly correct or in alignment with every life circumstance, rather they know that in order to achieve something they simply need to get started. Effective leaders are passionate, have a vision for their goal, and are willing to take significant risks and learn along the way. And if they make mistakes, which even they admit they do more than successes, they ask themselves the right developmental questions to learn from those mistakes. As a result, they are better, more experienced from what they learned did not previously work.

A few years ago, I actually designed and ordered thousands of t-shirts with the following quote: 'Opportunities are not seen with the eyes, they are seen with the mind.' And frequently, I still wear this shirt. Whether I am at the gym, on a boat, in a store, etc., people ask me 'Excuse me, but where did you get that shirt?' I love watching their responses when I smile and tell them to 'Visit my website and order one.' They usually respond with 'Seriously?' and with a tone of disbelief that I made the shirt. But regardless, they appreciate the positive mantra which the shirt displays. I wear the shirt as often as possible in hopes of initiating an inspirational conversation that awakens other's awareness that we can condition our belief system for success. It's not about me, it's about the meaning of the shirt and how others apply its interpretation to their life. It's about what we vision in life, not what we see.

I intentionally wrote this article for a specific purpose. For reasons which I do not understand yet, I have had an extremely high frequency of conversations with others in the past 2-3 months about mental conditioning, or success conditioning as I prefer to label it. During my seminars and with coaching clients, I share this concept of needing to <u>unlearn</u> certain things for success, rather than learn, and it sincerely seems to strongly hit home. I am finding that this 'theory' is changing people's lives not only because it is simple, but because it works and is having lasting, significant impact. <u>You do not need to wait any longer in order to accomplish that goal; rather, you simply just need to get started</u>.

What is it you have always wanted to accomplish? What is something on your 'bucket list' or 'vision board?' What are you waiting on?

If you are not somehow in process of working towards that goal, you are likely more creative in finding 'reasons' rather than 'results.' How is that working for you?

Again, to achieve the results you want, you no longer need to wait. Simply just get started. I have coached people who want to write a book, become a speaker, start a new business, get out of their 'rut', go back to school for a degree, geographically move, improve their relationships, etc. Yet with each person, they have initially convinced themselves that these objectives are only in the future and that they need more time to plan for designing the 'plan' or strategy. Beyond initiating the conversation with me, which is the first step, they do not feel ready to take that second step of action, the most important step of action.

I have experienced these folks have already convinced themselves, because of life-long mental conditioning, that they need to have a full-fledged business plan before putting rubber to the road and pursuing that new goal. Or, for other fabricated reasons made up in their mind, they feel they need to wait in order to have Planet Earth be better aligned with the sun. Their conditioned minds have ordered them to wait – and they listened. As a result, no results. Only hopes of 'someday.'

Well, I do believe that having a strategy is important and that timing is important. And I am proud of anyone who is cautiously taking a leap of faith outside their comfort zone which will significantly impact their life. I acknowledge that making a life change or committing to a goal of great magnitude takes time and careful consideration. But to be blunt, from my own life experience and after dozens of coaching conversations, talk is cheap and leads to nothing but inefficiency. I believe in results, not reasons. No one has to wait for anything – they just need to get started. As Tony Robbins says, "The road of 'I'll do it someday' leads to a town called nowhere."

I believe accountability coaches, better known as life coaches or success coaches, are needed by everyone. I have one myself who is a great friend and we hold each other accountable weekly to our previous goals and plans of action. My coach helps keep even me keep on track and he catches me if I start becoming distracted by other rabbits in the field. If you chase two rabbits, you'll catch neither. And when I report back about reasons rather than results, my coach calls me out on it. He's there to help ensure that my mind is focused on being programmed efficiently and effectively. Our relationship has helped me tremendously.

So in order for you to manifest any change in your life, you first have to know what the change looks like - 80% of achieving any goal is simply knowing what that goal is. After you know what it is you want, then simply get started. Do not wait. The longer you wait, the longer you wait! Develop a plan, fuel it with your passion, and expect to work hard. I can guarantee you that you will begin making positive change in your life that you will be proud of. Do not convince yourself that you need to wait any longer. The time is now - just get started!

SUCCESS LEAVES CLUES

Success does leave clues if we are patient enough to look for them. Sometimes they are hidden in small creative places and other times they are surprisingly right in front of our nose.

Recently, I went to the lake with my family. While we were all out on the boat together, I decided to go water skiing. As I began pulling out all the ski equipment, I realized we had the ski's and ski rope but unfortunately no water ski rope handle. Frustrated, I looked all over the boat to find a spare handle or at least something I could use as an alternate. Without a handle, I would have nothing to hold onto. Therefore, no skiing.

Everyone in my family had the same reaction, each in their own way, "Guess you have to wait until next time Kevin."

I love my family, but when I want to do something, I rarely ever like to 'wait until next time.'

So I pulled the boat closer to shore and quickly anchored.

"What are you doing?" they all asked me.

"I'm going to go get a rope handle," I said.

"What are you talking about?" my sister kept asking.

I said, "You'll see," as I dove into the lake and started swimming to shore. About 100 feet later, I was walking around the shoreline looking for pieces of wood that would substitute for a ski rope handle. Finally, I found one of perfect diameter but it was about two feet too long. I grabbed the piece of wood anyways and slammed it against another log, breaking it in half.

"There we go," I said. "Perfect. A brand new ski rope handle." I then swam back to the boat with one arm holding the new log handle. This all took maybe ten minutes.

When I got back onto the boat, my sister said, "You're crazy." Still catching my breath, I replied, "Good. Because now I can ski."

What was most powerful about what had happened was not what I said during those few moments. But rather, it was simply what I did. I didn't need to explain the concept of 'perseverance' or 'think outside the box' to anyone. I wasn't even trying to be a 'leader'. I just wanted to ski.

However, as I have reflected on this incident, I did hope they were paying attention to the unspoken lesson I was demonstrating to them. Whereas many people might accept certain conditions in life, I do my best to create the circumstances I want.

This topic is relative because it involves taking action to create the circumstances you want. Successful people, however you may define success, have a tendency to create ideal circumstances consistently. In fact, they expect to have to work hard to be successful and they learn from setbacks and failure more than anyone. The clue to their success is in their resiliency, adaptability, and vision to achieve a goal despite any setback or frustration. They view "Setbacks as Set-Up's!"

While I was water skiing with that obnoxiously awkward log as a ski handle, I saw my two nephews staring at me. One of them was actually laughing at me holding the log, pointing one hand toward me and the other covering his mouth in laughter. For me though, I hoped he would realize the deeper lesson being taught that day which is if something goes wrong or if he doesn't have something he needs, then all he needs to do is improvise. He just needs to find a way to make it happen.

> *If we desire strongly enough, we'll keep looking until we find it.*

If you are a parent, read this next quote closely a few times: "Children may not pay attention to what you say, but they sure will pay attention to what you do."

I sure hope my nephew paid close attention to what I did last weekend. Even on vacation you can learn a thing or two.

I'll admit that skiing with that small log hurt my hands. I wish I had gloves with me or sandpaper to smooth the edges of the rough wood. But I didn't. Days later, my hands are fine and I am typing this column. No harm done except a cute, interesting story.

And when I got back on the boat, I laughed when my mom asked me if I got any splinters. "A few," I responded. My sister called me 'MacGyver' the rest of the day as well. I kept thinking to myself though, "Good, that means it's sticking."

I'll appreciate being called MacGyver any day of the week.

> *Children may not pay attention to what you say, but they sure will pay attention to what you do.*

THE POWER OF PERSPECTIVE

Not too long ago, the airline I was flying on lost my luggage. I fly quite often and normally do not check any bags, but this particular flight was especially important. I was speaking at a 3-day association conference and had a keynote presentation each day. So I wanted to take extra suits and supplies to ensure I did not get caught wearing the same suit twice – call it a guy thing.

I waited and waited at baggage claim. Made a few friends but my luggage never appeared. Once reality finally defeated me and my hope sunk into frustration, I joined my new acquaintances at the 'lost luggage' counter. It appeared that indeed I was going to be at the conference wearing the same suit and shoes for 3 days.

As we made small talk in line at the counter and compared war stories of how our luggage mysteriously disappeared, our jaws dropped as we heard the anger coming from the couple first in line. The wife was crying and the husband was keeping himself from jumping over the counter to personally inspect the agent's computer. We couldn't help but overhear how their luggage was lost as well.

My new suits and shoes had nothing on their lost luggage – the luggage the airline lost was their DOG!

Moral of the story --- it could always be worse. Change your perspective to help change your outcome. The lens at which you see your situation is only that – a lens. So modify your perspective to change how you see things.

The genesis of the following quote comes from Dr. Wayne Dyer, inspirational speaker and author. He says, "You can change absolutely anything about your life when you first change the way you see it." How true. So much of life is how we react to what we experience. We cannot control everything that happens to us, but we can control our choices in response.

True story: I ran my first half marathon a few years ago. I was doing extremely well up until roughly mile 10. I only had a little more than 3 miles remaining, but somehow my right calf was cramping up and putting me in significant pain. After drinking some water, stretching and walking for a few moments, my pain seemed to be getting worse. Thoughts of quitting raced through my mind.

But then I thought of my friend Steve who is one of the most joyful, uplifting people I know. Steve is also a paraplegic and cannot feel any sensation below his waist. I thought of Steve as I was about ready to quit, and I reminded myself that Steve would love to feel the pain I was experiencing. He would give anything to have any feeling at all.

After I thought about Steve, my pain suddenly disappeared. In fact, the last mile of the half marathon was my best mile. I was almost able to sprint the last quarter mile and ended up beating my time goal of 1:50:00. By changing my perspective during that race, even when experiencing pain, I was able to shift my focus and still achieve the goal.

So you can you. It is just a matter of (1) intention and (2) choice. How intentional are you about wanting to understand and act upon this mental ability to control your perspective and emotions?

There is significant power in this capability that results in not just goal attainments, but also serenity and emotional intelligence. Yet unfortunately, most of us are not aware and spend most of our day simply reacting to what happens to us.

But not anymore – you are now more intentional about your perspective than ever before. You now understand that you possess an understanding of 'how' you see situations in life. When you cognitively recognize this ability and power, you will be able to see various courses of action, or reaction, that exists with each experience. As a result, you have 'choices' in how you choose to respond in any situation. Because you see various perspectives, you also visualize creative solutions. You are now more powerful than ever.

Simply changing the way we think about something can change not just how we react, but more importantly, the ultimate outcome. So be mindful of your perspective – be in control of your actions – be purposeful in your choices.

> *Be careful what you think, for your thoughts become your words.*
> *Be careful what you say, for your words become your actions.*
> *Be careful what you do, for your actions become your character.*

Oh, and remember my lost luggage story? They found my luggage that very next morning and delivered it to me at the conference. Shockingly though, the couple with the lost pet never saw their Sparky ever again.

So again, life is all about perspective. When you assume it is the worst, change your paradigm. Your seemingly tragic situation might actually help you count blessings.

THINK DIFFERENTLY TO ACHIEVE AMAZING SUCCESS!

'Thinking differently' is an essential and fundamental concept for living a successful, and more importantly, a fulfilling life. The way we think determines how we feel, and how we feel dictates how we act. Our thoughts manifest an outcome, and our actions and behaviors can be changed at any moment simply by recognizing the power of our thoughts.

No matter where you've been and where you are in life, today depends on you. Today depends on the choices you make right now. Today is the most important day of your life simply because you are exchanging a day of your own life for it. Therefore, choose to live it as if it was your last – it could be. Why not choose to live it accordingly, with passion and purpose? Why not choose to think differently and achieve amazing success?

> *If you do what you've always done,*
> *you'll get what you've always gotten.*

Here's an example: Are you familiar with the name Roger Bannister?

Roger was an amazing athlete who broke the 4-minute mile record in 1954. Up until that moment in history, it was thought humanly impossible that someone could run one mile in under 4 minutes. Both 'tradition' and experts claimed this coveted milestone would always remain and everyone believed it to be true. That is, until Roger Bannister.

When Roger broke the 4-minute mile record, he proved it could be done. Here is what is even more fascinating though - within one year following Roger's amazing accomplishment, several other individuals broke the same 4-minute mile record. Since 1954 -dozens more. How was this possible? What was the difference since then?

Here's the key point - the single reason why dozens of people were also able to break this record was because they *knew* it could be done. Roger proved to the world that the 4-minute mile barrier was only a mindset. It was only a mental limitation and boundary that he believed could be broken through. He *thought differently* than everyone else and resultantly achieved his dream and changed history.

Wouldn't it be amazing to live daily like Roger Bannister? Imagine for one moment that every limitation and obstacle you hear about or visualize can be broken through. Envision the achievement of breaking through a barrier which everyone else sees except you. Feel the fulfillment of living your dreams before you even embark on the journey towards them.

What limitations have you placed on yourself? What has someone told you could not be done and you believed them? What traditions have you accepted because no one has yet been willing to think outside the box or comfort zone?

The next time someone tells you that you cannot do something or that some task cannot be accomplished, I want you to remember Roger Bannister. I want you remember that Roger did what everyone said could *not* be done. And the moment he proved it could be done, he changed history. You are no different than Roger Bannister – you just have to <u>think differently</u>!

So when you hear the phrase, "we've never done it that way" or "that won't work," please remember the story of Roger Bannister. Then smile at whoever that person is and say "OK - thank you." Then proudly allow them to watch you do it.

There are hundreds of stories just like Roger Bannister's. Your story is next!

Below is another example demonstrating how powerfully important the concept of thinking differently truly is. This exercise is also a practical activity that you can share with anyone whom you feel needs motivation, or a kick in the pants, to think differently. Share it with a friend, your family, even with your colleagues at work to start your next staff meeting.

<u>Directions below</u>:

Closely look at the nine dots. Now with your finger or a pencil, simply connect all nine dots with four straight, lines while also keeping your hand/pencil on the paper. Do not continue reading until you have spent at least one minute trying to connect all nine dots!

● ● ●

● ● ●

● ● ●

Were you successful at connecting all nine dots with four straight lines?

If so, congratulations, *but* you probably have seen this exercise before! If not, you are not alone. I typically use this activity in my motivational presentations for college campuses and businesses. To date, out of hundreds of presentations, not one person has ever successfully completed this exercise who did not already know how to do it beforehand.

As you will soon see, in order to achieve the task you must "think differently." It seems rather simple, but I acknowledge that it can be extremely difficult to change the way we think about something. We literally have to reprogram our minds to accomplish a different result. The concept is simple – the application of it is not!

I hope you now understand that in order to achieve unique, breakthrough results and to truly lead a fulfilling life and make a difference, you must *think differently*. Only then, will you experience life and accomplish the dreams and goals you aspire to achieve and have the full potential for. The power of thought is one of the most important concepts you have control over.

Visit www.kevincsnyder.com/resources to view the strategy you would use to accomplish the task!

> *A great many years ago I purchased a fine dictionary.*
> *The first thing I did with it was to turn to the word*
> *"impossible," and neatly cut it out of the book.*
> ~ Napolean Hill, Think and Grow

PEAK PERFORMANCE
IN THE WORKFORCE!

Exit interview statistics from human resource professionals show that the number one reason employees leave their job is because they do not feel personally satisfied or rewarded with their work. Studies have alarmingly found that only 31% of all employees feel valued by their employer. However, for those individuals who did feel fulfilled and appreciated, only 14% were anticipating looking for a new position. Appreciation and motivation equals peak performance in the workforce!

Motivation is not only important in our personal lives, but it also is an underlying factor in our careers. The more fulfilled we are with our work, the more productive we will be. So whether you work for a company, own the company, or are the company itself, work gratification is the key to your success. Easier said than done though.

Do you know someone who feels 'stuck' in their job? Do you know someone who just does not like what they do? Of course you do. In fact, you see a picture of them in your mind right now. That person just might even be you.

So what can you do about it?

The solution for this feeling of being trapped and not feeling inspired and gratified by our work is quite simple. The remedy is in helping employees (and ourselves!) to identify and connect interests and skill sets to a strategic direction will improve productivity, morale, and the companies' bottom line. And as previously mentioned, it will also keep these employees from seeking other employment. This includes you!

> *Peak performance in the workforce is about tapping ourselves and our employees to connect who we are with what we do.*

Of course it is easy to confuse our identity with work. For example, think about what happens when you are introduced to someone you have never met. So many times, when we meet someone new we ask them, 'So what do you do?' Then they answer that robotically-posed question with a flat work title and company name. Chances are they did not even address what they do or why they do it. Three to five minutes later, your conversation is stale and you want to move on to someone else.

Instead, why not ask, 'So tell me why you do what you do,' or 'Tell me about yourself.' Those questions open up a much more profound discussion and meaning of who we are. This discourse also connects our work to purpose. And again, when we truly understand the meaning of what we do, we realize that why we do it is far more important. Unfortunately, this simple fact is rarely acknowledged. The exciting news is that you can change work attitude and performance by simply focusing on the purpose for it.

So the next time you meet someone new, don't ask them what they do. Instead, ask them why they do it. They might look at you odd at first, but chances are you will have a far more intelligent and purposeful discussion. Test it out and let me know how it works.

Again, for any company, by identifying and connect employee interests and skill sets to a strategic direction, enhanced productivity, morale, and the companies' bottom line will result. It will also keep these employees from seeking other employment. Think about it - peak performance in business, bottom-line productivity, and retaining top employee talent and clients revolves around the tone of inspiration set forth by its leader.

Why would an employee want to work for a manager or company who lacks purpose and vision? Moreover, what business owner or manager wants employees in their company who lack enthusiasm and direction?

For the business owner/executive:

Want your employees to be more productive? BE THE CHANGE you want to see. Talk to them about their interests and skill sets and how those qualities favorably impact your business mission. Yes – simple. But when is the last time you had this conversation? When is the last time you facilitated such an intentional discussion with your staff? Or maybe the person you need to speak with is yourself! Whether you have employees or not, is your genuine core and passion connected with what you do on a daily basis?

For the employee:

Want more from your work and feel untapped? BE THE CHANGE and talk to your supervisor about better connecting your interests and untapped skill sets with the business mission. Yes again – simple.

Research on leadership qualities of the most successful entrepreneurs suggests they all possess an INSPIRING VISION for what they wanted to accomplish. Meaning, they had a PASSION for not only _what_ they did but also for _why_ they did it. Their passion portrayed a 'strategic confidence', was magnetic to their followers, and fueled their own persistence until their goal was accomplished.

> *There is a reason why some companies and executives are extraordinarily successful.*

There is a reason why some companies and executives are extraordinarily successful. Think of someone in your life whom you feel is extremely successful? Vision that person in your mind right now and identify the top reasons why you believe they are so accomplished. If you were to write down those qualities they possess, I am confident that the person you described is PASSIONATE about their work. I would also place a large bet that this individual is inspiring to be around and has a deep understanding for the meaning of their work. In fact, their work isn't work. They are connected to why they do what they do.

Peak performance in the workforce is about tapping ourselves and our employees to connect who we are with what we do. The result is a manifestation of personal meaning, purpose, and an understanding of _why_ we do what we do. This intention is the secret to achieving greatness and being an inspirational leader, whether you have a prestigious title or not.

THANK YOU for reading this book. Your investment in yourself has already proven valuable and we are honored to be part of your journey. If any of the authors can assist you with being your coach or cheerleader, please feel free to contact them.

Sincerely,

Dr. Kevin C. Snyder

Kevin@InspirActiveSolutions.com

www.InspirActiveSolutions.com

About Kevin

Dr. Kevin Snyder is a motivational speaker and author with a passion for helping individuals take action to lead successful lives and achieve their fullest potential. He has spoken in all 50 U.S. states, has authored four books, and has recorded  two instrumental piano CD's. He is also a former staff member aboard Semester at Sea, a certified skydiver and scuba diver, a sailing enthusiast, and winner on the game show 'The Price is Right!'

Kevin is an adjunct faculty member with the Center for Creative Leadership (CCL) which is the global leader in executive education and training. His agency, Inspir-ACTIVE Solutions, specializes in developing custom-based keynotes and leadership development seminars to ignite employee motivation, satisfaction, workforce performance and enhanced bottom-line results. If your company or association ever seeks a dynamic keynote speaker, then consider Inspir-Active Solutions!

Kevin earned his Doctorate in Educational Leadership from the University of Central Florida, a Masters in Educational Administration from the University of South Carolina and a Bachelors in Marine Biology from the University of North Carolina at Wilmington. Contact him at:

www.InspirActiveSolutions.com

Kevin@InspirActiveSolutions.com

BECOME PUBLISHED IN A GROUP BOOK SERIES!

Everyone has a 'story' and we want yours! Our group book initiative, titled 'Leading the Way; Stories of Inspiration and Leadership' is always looking for inspirational, true stories focused on leadership, accomplishment and heart-warming sacrifice. Stories should be filled with such intense emotion that it captivates each reader and inspires them to live more fulfilled, intentional, and passionate life.

Authoring a book is an intense experience that requires countless hours of focused thought, disciplined writing, and repetitive editing. Many people have aspired to write a book – however, becoming an author is an accomplishment very few have ever achieved. Being published as a contributing author in our 'Leading The Way' projects will add further credibility to not only your resume vitae and professional experiences, but also to your personal fulfillment. All we need from you is your 'story.'

This is your opportunity to become a published author by submitting a chapter of content in lieu of hundreds of pages. Practically everyone I have encountered with a goal for authoring a book has never completed their dream because of one OR more combinations of these four (4) reasons: (1) not enough content to publish a full book, (2) too expensive, (3) they were quickly frustrated and confused by the hundreds of book publishers making false promises, and/or most commonly (4) they did not know how or even where to begin.

Authoring and publishing a book can be extremely difficult. The majority of work comes after the manuscript is written! The advantage to being involved with a future 'Leading The Way' group project will be that you will become an acclaimed author with credibility and product to market yourself and/or sell! In addition, the powerful concept of a group book is that other authors on the project will be marketing you wherever their books travel as well. The exposure and marketing for you is literally exponential and limitless! You will never know where these books travel and who will notice you as an author.

How you sell, market, and give away your books is your complete discretion! Use your books as 'thank-you's' for clients and those you have conducted business with, sell online during/after speaking events, gift as holiday and birthday items, or give as mementos for close friends and family. Regardless of who receives your book, they will be impressed with your product and persistence to see it through completion!

For more information, contact:

Kevin@InspirActiveSolutions.com or visit
www.BecomePublishedToday.com

SUCCESS IS NEVER PAVED!

Made in the USA
Charleston, SC
21 November 2012